**W9-AQR-136**

**Date: 3/9/18**

**J 975.8 YOM**
**Yomtov, Nelson,**
**Georgia /**

My United States

# Georgia

NEL YOMTOV

**Children's Press®**
An Imprint of Scholastic Inc.

**Content Consultant**

James Wolfinger, PhD, Associate Dean and Professor
College of Education, DePaul University, Chicago, Illinois

Library of Congress Cataloging-in-Publication Data
Names: Yomtov, Nelson, author.
Title: Georgia / by Nel Yomtov.
Description: New York, NY : Children's Press, an imprint of Scholastic Inc., 2018. | Series: A true book |
    Includes bibliographical references and index.
Identifiers: LCCN 2017025784 | ISBN 9780531231630 (library binding) | ISBN   9780531247143 (pbk.)
Subjects:  LCSH: Georgia—Juvenile literature.
Classification: LCC F286.3 .Y66 2018 | DDC 975.8—dc23
LC record available at https://lccn.loc.gov/2017025784

Photos ©: cover: Sean Pavone/Shutterstock; back cover bottom: Dmitry Kosterev/Shutterstock; back cover ribbon: AliceLiddelle/Getty Images; 3 bottom: David Grimwade/Alamy Images; 3 map: Jim McMahon; 4 left: WilleeCole Photography/Shutterstock; 4 right: LFO62/iStockphoto; 5 top: Rob Hainer/Shutterstock; 5 bottom: F11photo/Dreamstime; 7 center top: novikat/iStockphoto; 7 top: Jeffrey M. Frank/Shutterstock; 7 center bottom: SeanPavonePhoto/iStockphoto; 7 bottom: Brian Lasenby/Dreamstime; 8-9: SeanPavonePhoto/iStockphoto; 11: iofoto/Shutterstock; 12: Robhainer/Dreamstime; 13: John Spink/Atlanta Journal-Constitution/TNS/Alamy Images; 14: Mother Daughter Press/Getty Images; 15 bottom: jimkruger/iStockphoto; 15 inset: Bruce MacQueen/Shutterstock; 16-17: Ryan Murphy/Getty Images; 19: F11photo/Dreamstime; 20: Tigatelu/Dreamstime; 22 left: Atlaspix/Shutterstock; 22 right: trubach/Shutterstock; 23 center right: IrinaK/Shutterstock; 23 top right: StevenRussellSmithPhotos/Shutterstock; 23 center left: WilleeCole Photography/Shutterstock; 23 bottom right: LFO62/iStockphoto; 23 top left: Darryl Brooks/Shutterstock; 23 bottom left: Brian Zanchi/Shutterstock; 24-25: Lukas Uker/Shutterstock; 27: Marilyn Angel Wynn/The Image Works; 29: Everett Collection/Superstock, Inc.; 30 bottom: Prsima/Archive/Superstock, Inc.; 30 top: Jeffrey M. Frank/Shutterstock; 31 bottom left: North Wind Picture Archives/Alamy Images; 31 bottom right: Currier & Ives/The Granger Collection; 31 top right: Peter Probst/age fotostock; 31 top left: Atlaspix/Shutterstock; 32: inga spence/Alamy Images; 33: Bettmann/Getty Images; 34-35: Andre Jenny/Alamy Images; 36: Todd Kirkland/Getty Images; 37: Marilyn Nieves/Getty Images; 38: Tampa Bay Times/Lara Cerri/The Image Works; 39: CDC/Alamy Images; 40 inset: GBM/Shutterstock; 40 bottom: PepitoPhotos/iStockphoto; 41: ESB Professional/Shutterstock; 42 top: Everett Collection; 42 bottom right: Everett Collection; 42 center: AP Images; 42 bottom left: Photo12/UIG/Getty Images; 43 top: Flip Schulke/CORBIS/Getty Images; 43 center left: Rue des Archives/The Granger Collection; 43 bottom left: Hans Namuth/Science Source; 43 bottom center: Estate Of Evelyn Hofer/Getty Images; 43 center right: The Collection of the Supreme Court of the United States/MCT/Getty Images; 43 bottom right: Allstar Picture Library/Alamy Images; 44 center: Rob Hainer/Shutterstock; 44 bottom: Olga Popova/Shutterstock; 44 top right: North Wind Picture Archives/Alamy Images; 45 center left: Susan E. Degginger/Alamy Images; 45 top: Sean Pavone/Alamy Images; 45 center right: Elva Dorn/Alamy Images; 45 bottom: SeanPavonePhoto/iStockphoto. Maps by Map Hero, Inc.

All rights reserved. Published in 2018 by Children's Press, an imprint of Scholastic Inc.
Printed in North Mankato, MN, USA  113

SCHOLASTIC, CHILDREN'S PRESS, A TRUE BOOK™, and associated logos are trademarks and/or registered trademarks of Scholastic Inc.

Scholastic Inc., 557 Broadway, New York, NY 10012

1 2 3 4 5 6 7 8 9 10 R 27 26 25 24 23 22 21 20 19 18

**Front cover: A riverboat in Savannah**

**Back cover: Peach**

# Welcome to Georgia

## Key Facts

**Capital:** Atlanta

**Estimated population as of 2016:** 10,310,371

**Nickname:** The Peach State

**Biggest cities:** Atlanta, Columbus, Augusta

UNITED STATES

Georgia

## Find the Truth!

**Everything** you are about to read is true *except* for one of the sentences on this page.

Which one is **TRUE**?

**T or F** Georgia is the largest state west of the Mississippi River.

**T or F** There are about 42,000 farms in Georgia.

GEORGIA

PJF7188

FULTON

Find the answers in this book.

3

# Contents

THE **BIG** TRUTH!

Cherokee ros

## What Represents Georgia?

White-tailed fawn

Berry College

# 3 History

# 4 Culture

Miss Freedom

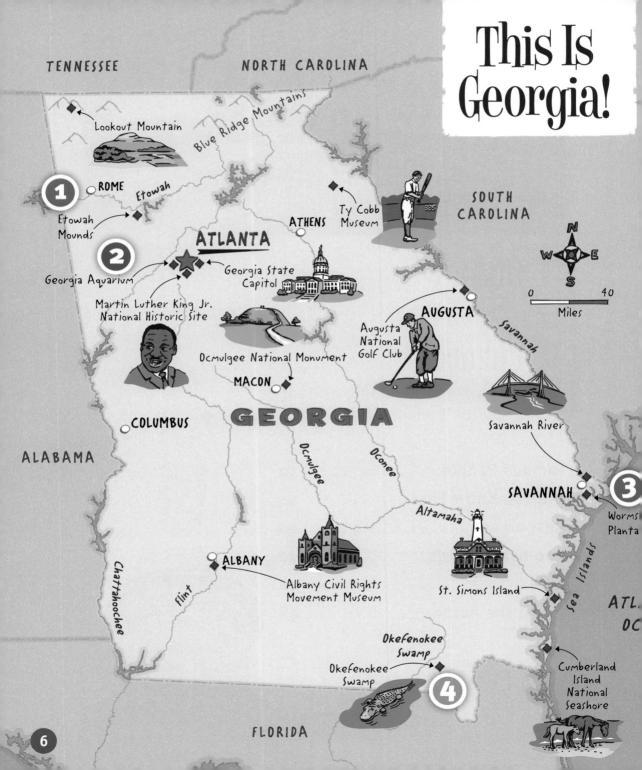

# This Is Georgia!

TENNESSEE

NORTH CAROLINA

SOUTH CAROLINA

ALABAMA

FLORIDA

GEORGIA

Lookout Mountain

Blue Ridge Mountains

**1** ROME

Etowah

Etowah Mounds

**2**

Georgia Aquarium

**ATLANTA**

Martin Luther King Jr. National Historic Site

ATHENS

Ty Cobb Museum

Georgia State Capitol

Ocmulgee National Monument

MACON

AUGUSTA

Augusta National Golf Club

Savannah

Savannah River

COLUMBUS

Ocmulgee

Oconee

Altamaha

SAVANNAH **3**

Worms Planta

St. Simons Island

Sea Islands

ATL OC

Albany Civil Rights Movement Museum

ALBANY

Chattahoochee

Flint

Okefenokee Swamp

Okefenokee Swamp

**4**

Cumberland Island National Seashore

N W E S

0    40
Miles

## ① Etowah Mounds

Located in Cartersville, this ancient site features six Native American earth mounds dating to about 1000 CE. A museum at the site shows how early Americans dressed and how they used local trees and plants for food and medicine.

## ② Georgia Aquarium

The Georgia Aquarium in Atlanta is the largest aquarium in the Western Hemisphere. More than 100,000 fish and other sea creatures make their home in the aquarium's 10 million gallons of water.

## ③ Wormsloe Plantation

A spectacular avenue lined with oak trees and Spanish moss leads visitors to the ruins of a historic 18th-century estate. The former home of Noble Jones, one of Georgia's first settlers from England, is the oldest standing structure in Savannah.

## ④ Okefenokee Swamp

The 700-square-mile (1,813-square-kilometer) swamp is a wildlife paradise. The vast, winding waterways are filled with snakes, alligators, hundreds of bird **species**, and plant life of all kinds.

Tallulah Gorge in northeast Georgia is 2 miles (3.2 km) long and nearly 1,000 feet (305 meters) deep.

# Land and Wildlife

Located in the heart of the Deep South, Georgia is one of the nation's most diverse states. From scenic peaks and cliffs to fertile valleys and breathtaking beaches, Georgia offers a wide variety of inviting landscapes. One of America's original colonies, Georgia's natural beauty is matched only by its long and inspiring history. For residents and tourists alike, Georgia offers plenty of adventure, excitement, and fun!

# Mountains, Rolling Hills, and Coastal Plains

Georgia is the largest state east of the Mississippi River and the 24th-largest state in the country. Tennessee and North Carolina form Georgia's northern border. To the east lie South Carolina and the Atlantic Ocean. To the south is Florida, and to the west is Alabama. Georgia is divided into three major land regions. They are the mountain region, the Piedmont Plateau, and the coastal plain.

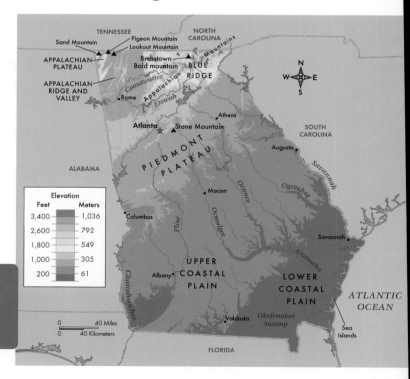

This map shows where the higher (orange and red) and lower (green) areas are in Georgia.

# Island State of Mind

The coast of Georgia stretches for about 110 miles (177 km) and includes dozens of barrier islands. They are called barrier islands because they form a protective barrier between the Atlantic Ocean and the mainland.

These islands were formed by ocean tides, wind, and currents moving ocean sand and river **silt** around. The ever-changing islands feature a variety of habitats, such as beaches, dunes, forests, wetlands, and reefs.

*Only four of the barrier islands are reachable by car.*

A waterfall is formed by the rushing waters of the Chattahoochee River, which runs along the border between Georgia and Alabama.

The mountain region lies in the northern part of Georgia. It includes the Appalachian Plateau and the Blue Ridge Mountains. The gentle rolling hills and fertile soil of the Piedmont Plateau lie south of the mountains. This area is dotted with rivers, waterfalls, and rapids. The coastal plain covers the entire southern half of the state. It includes the low-lying coastal region, the Okefenokee Swamp, and dozens of islands.

# Climate

Georgia has mild winters and hot, humid summers. The state's mountainous northern section is the coolest, and snow is a common sight during winter. Summers in the Piedmont are very hot and humid, with frequent thunderstorms. The climate along the Atlantic coast is hot during the summer and cool in the winter. In summer and fall, tropical storms bring heavy rains. **Hurricanes** occasionally hit the coast. They can cause serious damage.

Strong winds and heavy rain are common during Georgia thunderstorms.

MAXIMUM TEMPERATURE
112°F

MINIMUM TEMPERATURE
-17°F

# Plants

About two-thirds of Georgia is covered by forest. The state has about 250 different species of trees. White and scrub pines, red oaks, and buckeyes cover the mountain region. Yellow pines and maples grow throughout the Piedmont. Pecan trees grow in the south, with oaks and cypresses in the east. Other tree varieties include peach, cedar, sycamore, and hickory. Laurels, honeysuckles, Cherokee roses, and yellow jasmine are among the state's other beloved plants.

Peach trees produce beautiful pink flowers and sweet, juicy fruit.

# Animals

Georgia's mammals include bears, deer, foxes, raccoons, opossums, and beavers. Robins, blue jays, larks, cardinals, and brown thrashers

Red foxes can be found in Georgia's forests.

soar through the skies. Georgia's waters are home to trout, bass, catfish, dolphins, porpoises, shrimp, and blue crabs. About 80 reptile species, including poisonous snakes, are found in Georgia. The state's more than 80 amphibian species consist of salamanders, frogs, and toads.

Approximately 347 bird species can be seen in Georgia, including the blue jay.

The capitol houses the offices of the governor and other state officials.

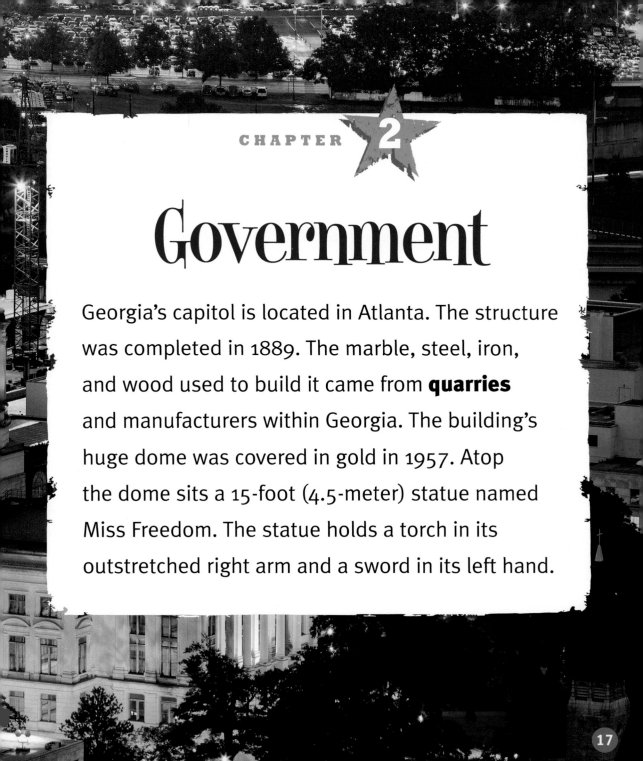

# CHAPTER 2

# Government

Georgia's capitol is located in Atlanta. The structure was completed in 1889. The marble, steel, iron, and wood used to build it came from **quarries** and manufacturers within Georgia. The building's huge dome was covered in gold in 1957. Atop the dome sits a 15-foot (4.5-meter) statue named Miss Freedom. The statue holds a torch in its outstretched right arm and a sword in its left hand.

Georgia's government is divided into three branches: executive, legislative, and judicial. The governor is the head of the executive branch. This branch oversees government agencies and proposes the state budget. The legislative branch is made up of the Senate and the House of Representatives. Its job is to make Georgia's laws. The judicial branch hears court cases and decides if state laws are legal.

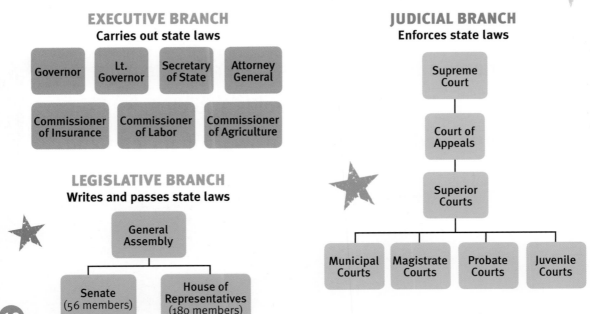

**GEORGIA'S STATE GOVERNMENT**

**EXECUTIVE BRANCH**
Carries out state laws

- Governor
- Lt. Governor
- Secretary of State
- Attorney General
- Commissioner of Insurance
- Commissioner of Labor
- Commissioner of Agriculture

**JUDICIAL BRANCH**
Enforces state laws

- Supreme Court
- Court of Appeals
- Superior Courts
  - Municipal Courts
  - Magistrate Courts
  - Probate Courts
  - Juvenile Courts

**LEGISLATIVE BRANCH**
Writes and passes state laws

- General Assembly
  - Senate (56 members)
  - House of Representatives (180 members)

# The State Constitution

The organization of Georgia's government and laws are described in the state constitution. This document also spells out the basic personal rights granted to the people of Georgia and the powers given to government officials. Since 1777, Georgia has had 10 state constitutions, second only to Louisiana, which has had 11. Georgia's current constitution has been in effect since 1983.

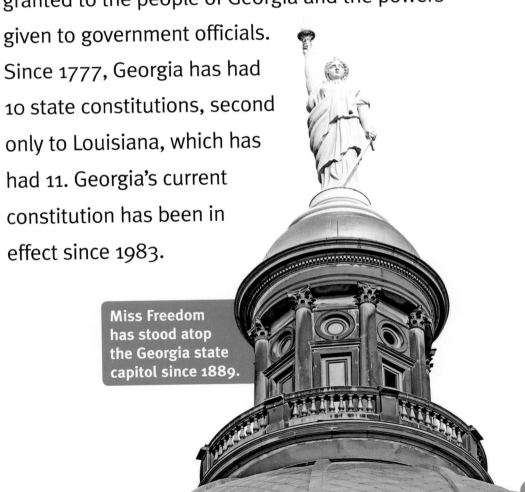

Miss Freedom has stood atop the Georgia state capitol since 1889.

# Georgia's National Role

Each state sends elected officials to represent it in the U.S. Congress. Like every state, Georgia has two senators. The U.S. House of Representatives relies on a state's population to determine its numbers. Georgia has 14 representatives in the House.

Every four years, states vote on the next U.S. president. Each state is granted a number of electoral votes based on its number of members in Congress. With two senators and 14 representatives, Georgia has 16 electoral votes.

2 senators and 14 representatives

16 electoral votes

Georgia has an above-average number of electoral votes.

# Representing Georgia

Elected officials in Georgia represent a population with a range of interests, lifestyles, and backgrounds.

## Ethnicity (2016 estimates)

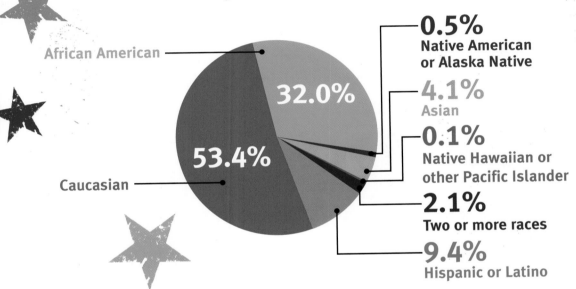

African American

Caucasian

**53.4%**

**32.0%**

**0.5%**
Native American
or Alaska Native

**4.1%**
Asian

**0.1%**
Native Hawaiian or
other Pacific Islander

**2.1%**
Two or more races

**9.4%**
Hispanic or Latino

**13.6%**
speak a language other
than English at home.

**63.3%**
own their homes.

**53.6%**
live in cities.

**85.4%**
of the population
graduated from
high school.

**28.8%**
of the population
have a degree
beyond high school.

**9.8%**
of Georgians were born
in other countries.

# What Represents Georgia?

States choose specific animals, plants, and objects to represent the values and characteristics of the land and its people. Find out why these symbols were chosen to represent Georgia or discover surprising curiosities about them.

## Seal

The three pillars on Georgia's state seal symbolize the three branches of government. The soldier with a drawn sword defends the constitution and its principles of "Wisdom," "Justice," and "Moderation." The date 1776 appearing at the bottom of the seal is the year the Declaration of Independence was issued.

## Flag

Georgia's state flag was officially adopted in 2003. The state coat of arms with the phrase "In God We Trust" appears in a blue square in the upper left corner. Thirteen white stars circle the coat of arms. The stars represent Georgia and the 12 other original states.

## Grits

**STATE PREPARED FOOD**
Popular throughout the South, this dish is made from boiled cornmeal.

## Largemouth Bass

**STATE FISH**
Georgians love fishing for this species in the state's many lakes.

## Green Tree Frog

**STATE AMPHIBIAN**
This small frog is a common sight throughout many of Georgia's forests and backyards.

## White-Tailed Deer

**STATE MAMMAL**
Georgia is home to about one million of these forest-dwelling mammals.

## Vidalia Onion

**STATE VEGETABLE**
This sweet yellow onion cannot grow anywhere other than in certain parts of Georgia.

## Cherokee Rose

**STATE FLOWER**
This white flower is famous for its pleasant scent.

Dinosaurs such as hadrosaurs, tyrannosaurs, and *Albertosaurus* once lived in Georgia.

# CHAPTER 3

# History

Millions of years ago, a tropical climate existed in the region that is now Georgia. The Atlantic Ocean covered most of the southeastern part of the state. During this time, dinosaurs and other prehistoric creatures roamed the land. Scientists have discovered the **fossils** of dinosaurs, giant woolly mammoths, camels, and ground sloths as tall as 20 feet (6 m).

# Native Americans

The first humans to live in present-day Georgia arrived about 12,000 years ago. These people hunted large animals such as **mastodons**. They also gathered nuts, berries, and fruits. By about 1000 CE, a group known as the Mound Builders lived in Georgia. They constructed large earthen mounds that were used as homes for rulers or for religious and burial purposes.

The Etowah Indian Mounds site near Cartersville is one of several locations where mounds can be seen today.

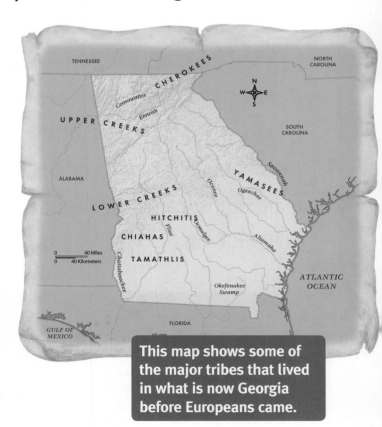

This map shows some of the major tribes that lived in what is now Georgia before Europeans came.

Creek people built homes from logs.

The Cherokee and Creek peoples are **descendants** of the Mound Builders. The Cherokees mainly lived in northeastern Georgia. The Creeks were more numerous and lived in large areas in the western part of the state. Both groups farmed, hunted, and caught fish and other seafood. Smaller Native American groups, such as the Hitchitis, Yamasees, and Tamathlis, inhabited other areas in Georgia.

# Enter the Europeans

The first European to arrive in Georgia was the Spanish explorer Hernando de Soto in 1540. Many Native Americans died in battles with de Soto's soldiers. Others died from diseases the Spaniards brought with them from Europe. Spanish explorers later set up forts and **missions** in Georgia. In time, the British drove out the Spaniards. By the early 1700s, pirates roamed Georgia's waters, attacking ships.

Some people believe that pirates buried treasure on the barrier islands!

This map shows the route taken by Hernando de Soto as he explored what is now Georgia.

In 1733, James Oglethorpe of England established a **colony** in Georgia. At first, slavery was banned in the new colony. But some colonists smuggled in African slaves to work on their farms. Cotton became the colony's most important crop.

The American colonies fought Great Britain for their independence in the Revolutionary War (1775–1783). After their victory, the colonies created a new nation, the United States of America. On January 2, 1788, Georgia became the nation's fourth state.

# From Civil War to Civil Rights

By the 1860s, slave labor had made many plantation owners wealthy. However, many people in Northern states wanted to end this horrific practice. During the Civil War (1861–1865), Georgia and other Southern states **seceded** from the Union. They fought to stop slavery from being outlawed, but were defeated. The war left Georgia in ruins. Factories and businesses were destroyed, and Atlanta was burned to the ground. It took years for Georgia to rebuild its economy.

# Timeline of Georgia Events

**1000 CE**
The Mound Builders erect large earthen mounds in Georgia.

**1540**
Spanish explorer Hernando de Soto reaches Georgia.

| ca. 10,000 BCE | ca. 1000 CE | 1540 | 1733 |
| --- | --- | --- | --- |

**ca. 10,000 BCE**
The first humans arrive in present-day Georgia.

**1733**
James Oglethorpe establishes a British colony in Georgia.

Although slavery in the United States had ended, African Americans in the South struggled to gain **civil rights**. Many black people were killed by white mobs. Countless others were prevented from voting. In the 1950s and 1960s, Atlanta-born Martin Luther King Jr. led protests to end the unfair treatment of blacks. By the mid-1960s, Congress passed laws to guarantee African Americans the same rights enjoyed by whites.

**1775–1783**
Georgia colonists fight in the Revolutionary War.

**1861–1865**
Georgia and the other Southern states secede from the Union and fight in the Civil War.

**1775–1783**  **1788**  **1861–1865**  **1996**

**January 2, 1788**
Georgia becomes the fourth state.

**1996**
Atlanta hosts the Olympic Games.

31

Farmers harvest tobacco on a Georgia farm.

## Georgia Today

Georgia's economy is one of the strongest in the nation. Huge companies such as Coca-Cola, Home Depot, and Delta Airlines are based in the state. Georgia's farm industry is a major producer of poultry, eggs, peanuts, and pecans. Atlanta has become the economic capital of the South. In 1996, the city hosted the Olympic Games. Georgia's scenic beauty and popular attractions also make it a popular destination for tens of millions of tourists each year.

# Julian Bond: Barrier Breaker

Julian Bond was one of Georgia's most influential leaders during the civil rights movement. Born in Tennessee in 1940, Bond attended Morehouse College in Atlanta. In 1965, he was elected to the Georgia House of Representatives. Other representatives, however, tried to block him from serving because he opposed the Vietnam War. The case went to the U.S. Supreme Court, which ruled in Bond's favor. He served 10 years in the House and was then elected to the Georgia Senate, where he served until 1986.

The Freedom Quilt Mural in Atlanta was created to honor people who have fought for freedom and equality in America.

# CHAPTER 4

# Culture

All across Georgia, people have many opportunities to enjoy the arts and culture of the Peach State. From museums and art galleries to world-class attractions, fairs, and celebrations, there's always plenty to delight in. And if you're traveling to Georgia from afar, you won't be alone: the Hartsfield-Jackson Atlanta International Airport handles more passengers each year than any other airport in the world!

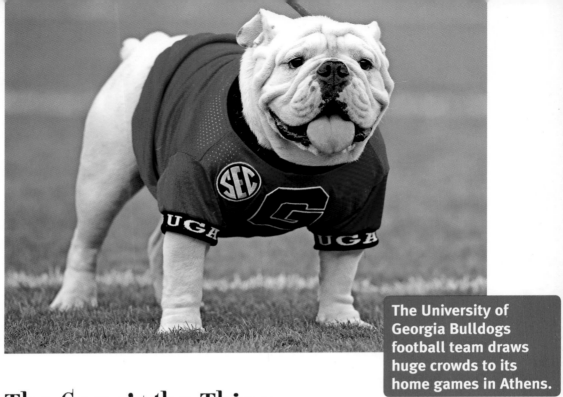

# The Game's the Thing

Atlanta is big on sports. Its Major League Baseball team, the Braves, plays at the brand-new SunTrust Park. The Atlanta Hawks and the Atlanta Dream play pro basketball at Philips Arena. Major League Soccer fans root for the Atlanta United Football Club at the Mercedes-Benz Stadium. The stadium is also the home of the Atlanta Falcons of the National Football League.

# The Arts

The Woodruff Arts Center in Atlanta houses three major cultural institutions: the High Museum of Art, the Alliance Theatre, and the Atlanta Symphony Orchestra. Popular Peach State authors include Atlanta's Margaret Mitchell, who won the Pulitzer Prize for *Gone with the Wind* in 1937. In rural Georgia, folk art is a thriving pastime. The state has also produced many talented musicians such as Ludacris, Usher, Ray Charles, and the rock group R.E.M.

Bike riders show off their Halloween costumes at the Little Five Points Halloween Festival and Parade in Atlanta.

# Making a Living

Georgians work in a wide range of businesses. With about 42,000 farms, agriculture is one of the state's leading industries. The honeybee industry is especially important to Georgia's economy. Honeybee farmers raise the insects to produce honey, beeswax, and other products. Many Georgians develop computer programs and other technology. Hundreds of thousands of people work in the state's energy and tourism industries. About 70,000 Georgians work for the federal government.

Beekeepers must wear protective clothing and be extremely careful when harvesting beeswax and honey.

CDC scientists in Atlanta wear protective clothing as they conduct tests on flu specimens.

# Health and National Security

Georgia is home to several important federal agencies and organizations that help keep Americans healthy and secure. The Centers for Disease Control and Prevention (CDC) is based in Atlanta. The CDC works to protect the health and safety of the public by studying disease and injury. Among the numerous military bases in Georgia are Naval Submarine Base Kings Bay, Moody Air Force Base, and Fort Benning.

# Good Eats!

Georgia has a reputation for its corn, apples, and blueberries. There are also the "three Ps": peaches, pecans, and peanuts. Other local favorites include barbecue, fried chicken, and fresh seafood. Brunswick stew—made with tomatoes, beans, okra, and other vegetables or meats—is said to have originated in Georgia. For dessert, those with a sweet tooth enjoy cornbread cake, pecan pie, and peach cobbler.

**Ask an adult to help you!**

## Cucumber Sandwich

Cucumber sandwiches are a favorite teatime snack throughout Georgia. These tiny nibbles are refreshing and easy to make.

### Ingredients

Mint leaves
Cream cheese, softened
White bread, thinly sliced

Cucumber, thinly sliced and drained on paper towels
Sour cream

### Directions

Mix the mint into the cream cheese. Cut the crusts from each slice of bread. Spread the cream cheese mixture on each slice. Top with a slice of cucumber. Plop a small scoop of sour cream on each cucumber slice. Enjoy!

# Georgia on My Mind

Fun and excitement await anyone who lives in or visits Georgia. Each January, Atlanta's Martin Luther King Jr. March and Rally celebrates the life of the famous civil rights leader. The Georgia Peach Festival held in Peach County each June offers parades, arts and crafts, and peach-themed products. The Yellow Daisy Festival in September at Stone Mountain showcases the creations of Georgia's artists and craftspeople. Get to Georgia for the must-see, must-do experience of a lifetime! ★

Children play at Centennial Olympic Park in Atlanta.

# Famous People

## Juliette Gordon Low

**(1860–1927)** a native of Savannah, founded the Girl Scouts of the United States of America in 1912. Originally called the American Girl Guides, it is now the largest educational organization for girls in the world.

## Carson McCullers

**(1917–1967)** wrote novels about small-town life in the Deep South. The Columbus-born author is best known for *The Heart Is a Lonely Hunter* and *The Member of the Wedding*.

## Jimmy Carter

**(1924– )** born in Plains, was the 39th president of the United States and the only Georgian to serve as president. Before being elected in 1976, he served in the Georgia senate and as governor. He was awarded the Nobel Peace Prize in 2002 for his work in human rights.

## Ty Cobb

**(1886–1961)** a native of Narrows, was one of the greatest baseball players of all time. He holds the record for the highest career batting average (.366) and won the American League batting title nine years in a row. He was inducted into the National Baseball Hall of Fame in 1936.

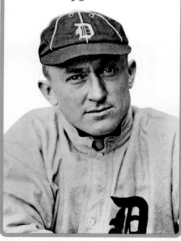

# Martin Luther King Jr.

**(1929–1968)** was the nation's foremost civil rights leader of the 1950s and 1960s. A Baptist minister born in Atlanta, he led a series of boycotts and marches to end racial segregation throughout the country. A believer in nonviolent protest, he received the Nobel Peace Prize in 1964.

# Clarence Thomas

**(1948– )** is the second African American to serve on the U.S. Supreme Court. A native of Pin Point, he is known for his conservative viewpoints and rarely speaks during lawyers' oral arguments.

# Ray Charles

**(1930–2004)** began losing his sight at the age of five. He learned how to play piano and emerged as a major pioneer of rhythm and blues music. He was born in Albany.

# Jasper Johns

**(1930– )** a native of Augusta, is an internationally renowned painter and sculptor best known for his abstract and pop art creations. His most notable painting, *Flag*—inspired by a dream about the American flag—was sold at auction for $36 million in 2014.

# Jessye Norman

**(1945– )** is one of the world's most famous opera singers. After she earned a master's degree from the University of Michigan School of Music in 1968, she moved to Europe and won an international music competition in Germany. She was born in Augusta.

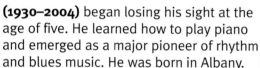

# Kanye West

**(1977– )** gained fame writing and producing hit songs for Jay Z, Alicia Keys, and other stars. He later became a critically acclaimed rapper himself and released several best-selling albums. He was born in Atlanta.

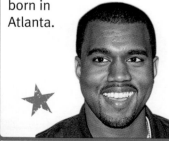

# Did You Know That ..

**18**
21

Hart County is Georgia's only county named after a woman. It is named for Nancy Hart, a heroine of the Revolutionary War.

In 1943, Georgia became the first state to lower the legal voting age from 21 to 18.

Berry College, in Mount Berry, has the largest college campus in the world. It covers more than 27,000 acres (10,926 hectares). That is about the size of 20,455 football fields!

ANTIGUA

10c

EDWARD TEACH (BLACKBEARD) AND PIRATE KETCH

Blackbeard Island, located along Georgia's coast, was named for Edward Teach, the notorious English pirate known as Blackbeard. Today, the island is home to a national wildlife sanctuary.

In 1829, Dahlonega in northern Georgia became the site of a major gold rush. Gold hunters headed to Georgia until gold was discovered in California in 1848.

The Varsity, located in Atlanta, is the world's largest drive-in restaurant. It can handle 600 cars and more than 800 people inside. About 30,000 people visit the Varsity every day.

There are more than 50 streets in Atlanta with "peachtree" in their names.

# Did you find the truth?

(F) Georgia is the largest state west of the Mississippi River.

(T) There are about 42,000 farms in Georgia.

# Resources

## Books

### Nonfiction

Cunningham, Kevin. *The Georgia Colony*. New York: Children's Press, 2011.

Hamilton, John. *Georgia*. Minneapolis: ABDO Publishing, 2016.

Kirchner, Jason. *Georgia*. North Mankato, MN: Capstone Press, 2017.

### Fiction

McCullers, Carson. *The Heart Is a Lonely Hunter*. Boston: Houghton Mifflin, 1940.

Walker, Margaret. *Jubilee*. Boston: Houghton Mifflin, 1966.

**Visit this Scholastic website for more information on Georgia:**

★ www.factsfornow.scholastic.com
Enter the keyword **Georgia**

# Important Words

**civil rights** (SIV-uhl RITEZ) basic rights guaranteed to all citizens, such as the right to vote and the right to equal treatment under the law

**colony** (KAH-luh-nee) a community settled in a new land but with ties to another government

**descendants** (dih-SEN-duhnts) your descendants are your children, their children, and so on into the future

**fossils** (FAH-suhlz) remains of an animal or plant from millions of years ago, preserved as rock

**hurricanes** (HUR-uh-kainz) violent storms with heavy rain and high winds

**mastodons** (MAS-tuh-donz) extinct animals distantly related to elephants

**missions** (MISH-uhnz) churches set up in foreign countries used for religious and humanitarian purposes

**quarries** (KWOR-eez) places where stone or sand is dug from the ground

**seceded** (suh-SEED-id) formally withdrew from a group or an organization, often to form another organization

**silt** (SILT) fine particles of soil that are carried along by flowing water

**species** (SPEE-sheez) groups of similar living organisms that can breed with other members of the group

# Index

Page numbers in **bold** indicate illustrations.

# About the Author

Nel Yomtov is an award-winning author who has written nonfiction books and graphic novels about American and world history, geography, mythology, sports, science, careers, and country studies. He is a frequent contributor to Scholastic book series.